THE MAKING
OF STONES

Dear Lizzie

THE MAKING
OF STONES

*" Never run from
anything immortal —
it only attracts their
attention."
Love you, beautiful
spirit.*

ANDREA EAMES

A Eames

ISBN: 1522755683
ISBN 13: 9781522755685

For Aaron
and Sarah
and Jenna:

who, together,
helped make 2015 into poetry
out of pain.

CONTENTS

IF YOU LOVE ME

I will be too much, I promise;
and I promise I will be faithful
in ways you do not want, or expect.
My mouth is sullen and hungry,
and you must have all of it or none;
teeth, tongue, palate, one animal
sour and demanding and devouring.
In return, I will unskein myself,
unskin myself and spread my pelt,
taut and tent-pegged, to hammock you.

I will swaddle you and feed you
my love in pieces; plug your mouth,
make it milk-drowsy and morphiate.
I will suffocate and smother you
with my perfumes, sweet and foul both,
and I will turn your stomach,
and breathe myself through your lungs
and weigh them in my two hands
to feel them swollen and surrendered;
and I will eat each of your breaths with

the spoon of my tongue, and I will
unswallow them back to you as kisses.
I will suck the ichor from your eyes.
I will uproot your hair by the handful
and use it in unspeakable rituals.
I will chew the parings of your nails.
I will not let any part of you go to waste;

my disgust is pungent as my pleasure
and you shall have more than enough
of both. Your repugnance is sweet, and

I will not meet your mother
and she will not approve of me.
If you love me, it will choke you
until you are gagged and gagging
and I will not accept your sipping,
your timidity. Gorge yourself on me.
Be engrossed. Be repelled, if you must.
And, if you shuffle backwards after,
husked and giggling, then you,
my dear, were not worth the tasting.

VALENTINE

I do not wear my heart
on my sleeve
but smeared on my face

like Mum's
lipstick
stolen from her drawer,

swivelled from its gold tube,
a bright and waxy finger,
admonishing;

wagging in my face;
tsk tsk, not for you
little girl.

I want
the smooth-painted mouth
inviting kisses

but I want too much.
No decorous shape
but a melting scrawl

coloured outside the lines.
Too red on my cheeks,
my hands.

It is too much.
I am
too much;

too eager
to love
to be loved.

THE MAKING OF STONES

My love,
form slowly;
form secret and swelling,
buried deep and hidden;

hardening,
waiting.

You are
palm-cupped heaviness;
a pocket universe,
mass and matter dense-packed,
filled to bursting.

You are a lump in the throat, never swallowed.

Form egg-like and secret;
form tumorous;
form slowly.

Wait
Wait

Form slowly,
buried deep and hardening;

form round and smooth.

You are a lesson in yearning;
a lesson in patience.

HAIKU

I must confess, I
am tired of being human;
tired of the stirring

of primordial
urges, those thick, soupy tides
sluggishly rippling,

blood-warm and ugly.
Meanwhile, the world ages and
sags, damp with wanting;

and so I retreat —
eat a hole in an apple
and curl up inside

in the crisp and cool
in the hollow bald chambers
echoed and empty.

I must confess, I
am tired of being human
so tired of needing.

THE SEA-WIFE

I

You must pay her dearly for it, the witch.

It is no small thing
to bring a wife from the waves —
to slipe her from the foam,
mottled and gleaming,
glossy as sea-glass.

A seal is not a romantic creature.
Almost liquid underwater, on land it is
lumbering and lumpen,
a swollen parody of animal,

but, witch-sung, it finds inside itself
the girl-form there,
white and slick as coconut
coaxed from the bristled husk.

Slid from her skin she emerges,
shivering and damp and blinking
at this sudden narrowing of her senses;
the sudden weakness of her body,
unmuscling.

You catch her hands and name her parts

and she tries to walk
on feet as good as bound
by the memory of fins.

You will marry her, that is the bargain.
She is alien, unmarred.
She is musk-oil beneath your fingers
salted and smelling of the sea;
she yields liquor clear as an oyster's
beneath your press and stroke.
She is mute and gentle,
biddable and wilted,
unnamed, untouched by any but you.

This is your reward, then, for the price you paid:
a girl new-shucked,
a girl you can name.

The magic can only be undone
by the discarded skin,
precious and repulsive at once.
It will dry and harden,
and stink,
and shrink,
curling at the edges;
an unpleasantly animal reminder.

You tuck it under your arm
to be hidden
and forgotten

lest she find it hanging
with the uncured meats

and take it down from its hook
and ease those unfamiliar feet
back into the stiff hide.

You will know it is coming,
all through the long days of your marriage
as you teach her to herself;
you were warned of her growing melancholy,
her silences — it is the same with all the sea-wives,
you were told, but you thought she would be different,

that she were bound to you by more than witch-song
and that you would somehow out-dazzle the power
of her old body and the sea together,
that she would forget how one fit within the other,
a drop of ink in an inkwell.

You will know it is coming,
that day when she goes hunting
through the house, never wholly hers,
and opens all your doors to find her poor pelt.

She will run to the ocean.
She will pull the rough, rubbery thing over her head
like the silk evening gown
she will no longer need
and stitch it closed with her own bare fingers
as blood re-pools
and the lace of veins is re-webbed
and she is re-sealed,
and matted fur springs to seashined life.

One day she will wash up, perhaps,
with the driftwood and bladderwrack,
guarded by gulls,
and you in your long grief will not recognise her,
but kick at the carcass as you pace the sand
and call to the ocean
hoping by blind luck to strike the one right song
to bring her home.

II

Not for the squeamish,
this self-skinning;
I am belly-up and bloated,
spread-legged and ready for the knife.

Knowing, my skin
shrinks about the bones

the sea throws a tantrum
clinging to my hand
begging me to stay.

But I have made up my mind.
I slit myself from throat to tail
from gullet to udder
and part like lips;
inside, the blubber,
the guts bulbous and gathered,
have become girl-child
willing and naked.
I am degloved
unmuzzled
flayed bare to the harsh salt
I can thumb the gentle hollows of my joints

and I step free
white and weak and staggering
white as a sapling peeled back
weak as the bare wrists of lilies
feet so tender
the sand alone raws them;

no longer animal
but manageable, compact,
unsullied
for you.

The pelt slumps, unbreathing.

Hide that bristle-haired mess,
that indecent, suffering skin-sack
before I am tempted
to shrug it back on:

scrape out the fat
spoon out the curd
and leave it
stiff and drying
stiff and dulling.

It strains after me
bereaved,
and bestial.

III

I did not ask you
I did not.

You say you do not blame me;

so, then,
quit your puling,
your belly-aching.

I did not know, when you stepped from your skin,
when I named you, and brought you home,
how sad and seeping you would be, how slumped
and melancholy, once the novelty wore off
for us both.

Enough weeping and wringing of hands.
Enough of your whining.
I was not the one who sung you out.
We are bound by the same spell;
I am as much a prisoner as you.

Give me my grief early;
you hold it over me,
your bristled coffin,
your magicked skin,
your soft and soggy yearnings.

You threaten me with the water,
with your seal-self.
At night you mouth your pillow, open-eyed,
with gormless gulpings,

soaking your story into the stuffing,
souring the linens with your nighttime breath
and murmurs, and mewlings,
and I have to lie there and listen.
I remember the peeled white of you
when you first stepped out;
your long virgin limbs, your never-tangled hair
your eyes, still part-seal, black and soft.

You have wilted;
still beautiful,
but sagging at the window, staring at the sea
with those black eyes, dumb and animal,
and I think of other girls, born girls,
freckled or browned or gingered in the hair,
less lovely than you, but less trouble.

Your shed skin; you bundled it into my arms
like an infant, and made me hold the stink of it;
it gloved my fingers
with an unsettling scent.
You asked me to hide it
you said you would be too tempted.
I can smell it on you still.

I have not hidden it all that well;
you could find it, if you really looked,
if you kept the place tidier
if you were more attentive in your duties.
Give me my grief early, then,
so that I may mourn you —

I am mourning you now.

THE THINNEST SKIN

A kiss is a thing we make, we two.
We form it round and supple, shapely;

we hold it suspended between us,
trapped and fluttering, in potentia.

That thinnest skin, taut and tearable,
with eager blood that colours and warms,

with webbed blood so finely netted —
the warp and weft of it, fine-woven,

knitted up in bright vermilion —
trapped in the subtle lines of the mouth.

A thing that we make; a tender theft.
I am sorry. I am not sorry.

BASOREXIA

No one
has kissed me mid-sentence;
kissed me at midnight.

I wonder if they
ever
think of it

as,
shamefully,
I do.

I feel my own mouth
warmed and waiting,
heavy

with waiting.
It is naked,
parted.

You have a wonderful
vocabulary
someone said.

I love
your mind,
the things you say.

But
I speak those things
with my mouth.

MY MOTHER TAUGHT ME

My mother taught me that men are important
and that they have needs needier than ours, and more pressing,
and that they have already been forgiven, by some ancient arrangement.
I am Eliot's patient, etherized; *undress to your comfort level* you say
and so I will unbutton my skin at the navel and slough it,
wrinkled and damp as bedsheets, so that it may be discarded
and I can butterfly myself upon the table, flayed throat to womb.
Do you enjoy a firm pressure? Exposed, unborn-me curls up tight,
strung from its own umbilicus, fists to ears, twitching.
Skinless, I am gilled and fish-finned,
or I am an oyster, bearded and loose-lipped and demanding,
all belly and gape and guts—or I am water, spread smooth and silken
as fabric on a cutting board, scissored by sharp-nosed boats, pleated at the shore
in neat, ribboned lines. Or I am finger-furrowed, pored over stitch by stitch
and felt between the fingers to determine my quality and weight.

I am imagining it. This is not happening, not really.
I imagine things all the time and they seem so real
but men tell me they are not, and my mother taught me that men know
what is real and what is imagined, and this is on par
with my dreams of spiders and losing my teeth.
I was right, you have not noticed unborn-me, as other mouths
open hot beneath your hands, between my legs, in my armpits;
slitting my throat in a toothless unsmile.
All the while, your crouched toad nudges at my crown, knuckling and fisting,
nosing into my bristled hairs, *a firm pressure,*
and the oils of my scalp sprout against it and my skull is wet.
Toothy toad, eat me out hollow;
lick the belly-bowl clean of its pap.

I envy you your cunning teeth and tongue. Mine are ineffective
despite my million mouths, and all I can do is swallow
and you say *You hold a lot of tension in your jaw.*

I press myself on you.
Take more, take another helping, take a larger helping.
You are skin and bones, I need to put some meat on you;
I break off pieces of myself; I soak them in milk, to soften and offer.
I will even chew them for you, if you wish, mumbling them from my mouth
to yours
because I am here to nourish you, all of you, whether you ask it or not.
You have spooned them out, my sweetbreads and offal and the good
fleshy parts,
and you have suckled my marrow and left me wholly plumbed,
and numbed, and comically rebuttoning myself in all the wrong holes.
The unborn-me is safe, too small and tough, but the rest is sour soup
and you rub your completion into my hair. I do not blame you and I am
not angry.
I am an invitation, and you cannot be faulted for accepting me —
because *I undressed to my comfort level* and because *I like a firm pressure*
and because you were hungry and my job is to feed you, all of you,
and because my mother taught me that men are important.

KISS

I feel your kiss
coalesce;

part me
with your tongue,

laparascopic.

You need
so little
so small
an opening
and you are
inside

I feel it

where I shouldn't;
where it's not.

I am sipped like pollen,

every kiss cloacal;
more than mouth
more than soft

as
all-petalled

it opens to
the shuddered centre

a wincing red.

BODYSURFING

The rush of it
the cold sluice
the grit

I am jackknifed and tumbled

The white teeth of it
the roil
the fizz and burn
the seething mess
lungfuls of it.

Blood is dark in my head;
water shouts in my ears, wide-mouthed.

Fingers tugged from hand
hand from wrist
wrenched by the froth and churn of it.

Underfoot, the sand is a ridged palate
licked by tough tongues of water;

I stand breath-strained

from a caul of wet, reborn.

I FUCK LIKE I THINK

I fuck like I think
too much
and too quickly

and

I fuck like I eat
not enough
or all at once.

My two dank tunnels
are hungry;
they meet in the middle
in the gut
sour and corrosive.

I am all hole
and
turned on the spit
of those two most accommodating organs;
made to encompass
to envelop
to suck and swallow.

Is that a problem
for you?
That I am greedy?
Or that I am smiling?

MY BODY

(*after Mary Oliver*)

My body
is more than a metaphor

but I hang meaning from it
like rags from a clothesline.

All kinds of clever things
can be said,

ridiculous comparisons—
it is nothing but

a nest of nerve-endings,
a conspiracy of sense,

blind, insistent,
nosing for warmth.

The soft animal
who wants what she wants

and wants what she shouldn't,
and wants

and wants.

RIP TIDE

You almost drowned;
tugged under, kicking at the current's eager hand
as it unzipped the ocean
exposing its hunched sandback

like the time you helped your mother
dress for a party
and were startled by her paleness
and the easy slide of the fastening
and how her skin snagged so neatly
                              between the metal teeth.

You staggered from the tide, hauled free,
and the sea closed up behind you
with a fine white seam.

THE GIFT

I gave you something
precious
to hold;
use both hands, I said.
Do not tremble.
Keep it steady.
Keep it sacred.

I have made it for you.
I have kept it secret,
curled myself around it,
let it form and harden
into lucence
in the spoon of my spine
and the tines of my ribcage.

It is fragile.
It is tender.
You took it,
my gift,
with thanks;
to pocket,
to treasure.
I imagined it snugly
nestled, warm against hip
and skin.
I imagined you palming it,
nursing its contours,

(I laugh at myself)
almost unbreathing,
rapt with its worth.

And then one day
I asked
to see it.

See what?
There's nothing, you said
and spread
your hands;

nothing there.

LITHOPAEDION

I

You only noticed when your stomach ached
a dark, cumbrous ache; malevolent fist
thrust downward. On the X-ray, a sour lump;
an ammonite hunched and sucking its thumb,
face melted as wax, a nub of a nose,
bones hollow as birds', fontanelle gaping.
Human, but not; just enough to disgust.
An effigy, noble as a cherub,
in its own sere, blood-formed sarcophagus.
A lithopaedion — a stone baby.
A medical opposite-of-marvel.
The doctors and nurses are delighted.
This is very rare. Almost un-heard-of.
Very few cases have been reported.

II

The earliest documented was French;
one Madame Chatri, butterflied open,
autopsy and delivery in one.
Sacre bleu, mon dieu, they probably said,
and they cracked the stone baby like a nut.
They published the story and her picture—
the madame and her ossified offspring—
or, not her picture, but something like it;
ripe woman, pornographic and sprawled loose
beside the wizened bundle of her child;

a stone fruit beside its hard, wrinkled pit.
The foetus was sold, passed from hand to hand,
was plinthed and displayed in a museum
and disappeared, stolen or lost, perhaps.

III

Once this blood was red and hot, spiderwebbed
under tender skin, flushed and quickening.
Once there were eyes, blind and wetly staring.
Once there was tongue, toe, throat, a heartbeat. Now
it's preserved *in potentia*, polished,
as a pearl in an oyster's fishy folds.
The correct term is calcification:
the body protects itself from decay,
serves a death notice, constructs its gravestone.
We unexplain with myth and medicine—
the mother, like Medusa, is to blame
we say; with her coldness, frigidity
she fossilized it, entombed and unwombed,
mummy-fied it to keep it safe, unborn.

IV

Maybe it's hereditary, this sickness —
Mum was in the hospital for so long.
A pregnancy, ectopic. Egg-topic;
her eggs were scrambled—no womb at the inn.
Your brother or sister, hatched too early
became a red trickle, siphoned and swabbed.
You keep your secret, you the stone baby,
swaddled in calcium, fossilized milk,
carrying your own foetus; nesting dolls,

one curled sleeping, snug within the other.
You are better this way, dead and perfect.
A real child would be furious, squalling;
no longer a beautiful sacrifice
but grossly bloated and fattened with life.

V

Listen. Though this is a rich tradition,
and the statue is blameless and perfect,
you can choose the chaotic child instead;
as if Madame Chatri unzipped herself
before the doctors got her, shucked herself,
left the shell hollow and desecrated,
cradled the grisly lithopaedion,
larval and tender; loved it back to life.
Listen. You can do the same, it is time.
Wake it up, although it will be frightened.
Warm it between cupped hands; blow gentle breath,
soften it with handling, ply and form it,
name it; remind it you are its mother.
Say you are sorry. Say you are sorry.

PROSPECT

Now
that they have settled—unmoving, unmoved —

I sit and sieve
what is valuable
what is rare
from the sediment;

hoping for a treasure,
a truth.

Shards dull or bright,
I winnow them
bowl by bowlful
searching for
the shining ones.

I must be careful
because
I want
so badly
to believe.

I find
so many
and

so many
are dear impostors,

beloved lies,
gleamed by the water
into preciousness

polished by the water
into radiance,

shining pyritic.

And I love them,
false as they are.

Let me keep just a few,
please.
Let me keep a palmful,
glimmering and dense.

Let me pretend
they are real.
What harm will it do

to anyone
but me?

HIGHCLIFFE BEACH

A beach here is
a stinking, gravelled sedge,
all bladderwrack and froth

and the ocean is brown broth

and, in our laughing panic,
we can barely tread water through
the conspiracy of weed

as,
tender and tentacled,
it eases flabby arms about our waists,

snares our limbs,

and we imagine
exchanging them, mermaid-like, for
the rough cutlery of claws
serving up the seabed
in impolite mouthfuls.

COMING

I hunch on your fist
avid and blinking
all clutch and sulk

and lift and settle;
my kerfuffle of feathers
oiled to the tips.

You have trained me to your hand;

before you, I did not
come when called.

When you fly me,
I am a weapon
I rattle like chain mail

high-flown and hunting,
I am a predatory smudge
in the shivering sky.

You have learned to read
the tilt of my head,
the cant of my hunger.

But you are a kind master.
You let me have my pleasure,
such as it is;

you loose me from the glove
you coax me away
then home.

I have learned your hand,
but you have not tamed me—

you take the risk, each time,
that I may hook a tree branch and hunker,
sullen and glowering.

I have learned to come, and come,
and, for now, I am content

but one day

I may knife my flight upward
and leave you to stare.

EVENING

(after Sara Teasdale)

I have smoked through my friends, as they say,
left them lipstick-rimmed, exhausted, stubbed out.
I have burned the candle at both ends, as they say,
wasted the wick,
am at the end of my rope, as they say, drawn taut,
and I am tired of this particular hurt, it is boring.

There is no numb. The world itches and raises welts
but my whorish senses insist on loving all of it at once,
cramming it wherever it will fit, greedy for this evening
candled by fireflies,
haunted by deer, arrowhead hooves neat-pointed
as they ankle through long grass brushed back.

The dog shoulders forward, eager and seal-sleek
and I can manage this, moving a body through the world,
drunk on my own skin. It is greedy, it is selfish
to take such pleasure
in my aliveness, the sweet heft of my living self,
the fireflies, the deer, the dog, the dampened air,

while at the same time hoping there will be
some shining strange escape prepared for me.

EMBRYO

Hello, tadpole;
an egg-smooth hammock
rocks like a lullaby
your unformed soul.

My how you've grown. You learned to swim.
How brave,
ready to flick your tailed, slick
body into the acid world, too bright.

Here's a thought;
would you rather stay dim,
mole-nosed and velvety in the dark,
or nudge towards the light?

ACKNOWLEDGEMENTS

I found poetry again this year—or, as it rather tartly suggests (as it reads over my shoulder; poetry is not known for its social niceties), I started to pay attention again after a long period of being rather dense. Thank you so much to David, always, who puts up with an awful lot and married himself to a writer, which on its own is deserving of praise and pity; to Sarah Kate Hackley, Aaron Glover and Jenna Martin Opperman, for reading my work and trusting me with theirs; to Louis Rakovich, who designed the perfect cover, and to Inge V. Skelly, who gave me permission to use her beautiful photograph; to Bedpost Confessions, for giving me the courage to stand in front of an audience and say things that would horrify my parents; and to that part of me who waited, however impatiently, for me to write these things down.